WOMEN IN HISTORY

19th CENTURY AMERICA

FIONA MACDONALD

Chrysalis Children's Books

This edition published in 2003 by
Chrysalis Children's Books
The Chrysalis Building, Bramley Rd, London W10 6SP

ISBN 1 84138 886 6

British Library Cataloguing in Publication Data
for this book is available from the British Library.

Series editor: Claire Edwards
Series designer: Jamie Asher
Cover designer: Keren-Orr Greenfeld
Picture researcher: Diana Morris
Consultant: Kate Moorse

Printed in Hong Kong
10 9 8 7 6 5 4 3 2 1

Picture acknowledgements:
Corbis-Bettmann: front cover cr & b, 1, 3r, 5t, 6b, 12t, 13b,
16, 17b, 19t, 22b, 23t, 26, 28, 29b, 31b, 32, 33t, 33b, 35b,
37, 39b, 40, 41, 43c, 43b, 44t, 44b, 45b.
Hulton Getty: 18, 27b, 29t, 43t.
Museum of the City of New York/Bridgeman Art Library: 24.
Peter Newark's Pictures: 3cr, 4, 5b, 7b, 8t, 8c, 9t , 11t, 19b,
20t, 20b, 21t, 21b 30, 36.
North Wind Picture Archive: front cover cl, back cover t & b,
3l, 3cl, 3c, 9b, 10, 11b, 13t, 14, 15t, 15b, 17t, 25t, 25b, 27t,
31t, 34, 39t, 42, 45t.
Oberlin College Archives: 23b.
Private Collection/Bridgeman Art Library: 7t, 8b, 38.
Smithsonian Institution, Washington D.C./Bridgeman
Art Library: 35t.

CONTENTS

A new nation

The United States of America was still a new nation in 1800. Since about 1600 most of the east coast of North America had been ruled as colonies by countries in Europe, especially the British. But by the late 1700s the British colonies were angry at having to pay British taxes and wanted the freedom to govern their own lands.

Revolution

In May 1775 people from all 13 British colonies met in Philadelphia, to discuss what to do about British rule. They decided that they would not accept it any longer. But Britain would not let its American colonies go free. Fighting broke out between the colonists and British troops. It continued until 1783, when Britain was defeated. The 13 colonies joined to form an independent republic – the United States of America.

We hold these truths to be self-evident, that all men are created equal, that they are endowed by their Creator with certain unalienable Rights, that among these are Life, Liberty, and the pursuit of Happiness. That to secure these rights, Governments are instituted among Men, deriving their just powers from the consent of the governed.

FROM THE DECLARATION OF INDEPENDENCE

In 1776 representatives of the rebel American colonies signed the Declaration of Independence. In it, they demanded human rights and individual liberty, and proclaimed that they would no longer accept British laws.

Abigail Adams (1744–1818), wife of the second president and mother of the sixth president of the United States. She ran the family farm and brought up five children while her husband John Adams was away on political campaigns. People said that he often depended on her wise advice.

Remember the ladies

Many American women were worried by this 'men only' attitude. They shared American men's wish for independence, and their respect for human rights. But they wanted the chance to take part in the new American nation, in helping to develop its schools, hospitals, businesses and farms. In 1776 Abigail Adams wrote to her husband John Adams, who was away helping to draw up the Declaration of Independence. She asked that, 'In the new code of laws which I suppose it will be necessary for you to make, I desire you would remember the ladies... Do not put such unlimited power into the hands of husbands.' But John Adams, who later became second president of the USA, wrote back, 'As to your extraordinary code of laws, I cannot but laugh.'

Human rights

The Declaration of Independence began with a brave statement about human rights. The soldiers and idealists who led the fight for independence wanted their new nation to be a land of freedom and equality. In 1787 they drew up a new Constitution (law code). It gave all men in the USA the right to carry weapons, the right to free speech, and the right to follow their own religion. But it did not mention women's rights. In fact, the Constitution gave men complete control over all their property, which included their wives and children.

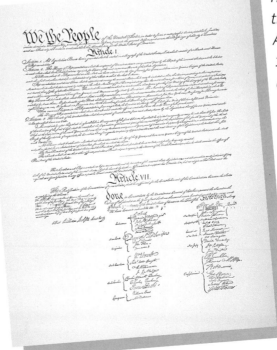

The Constitution of the United States of America, agreed in 1787, laid down all the basic laws by which the nation is still governed. Over the years, other laws have been added in the form of amendments (extra rules) on special topics, such as the abolition of slavery, or women's right to vote.

5

From farms to factories

Between 1800 and 1900 the United States was an exciting place to live. It was the fastest-growing, fastest-changing country in the world, and people there were inspired by a great sense of adventure and opportunity. Hopes were high. Everything seemed possible in the new 'land of the free'.

> *Americans have two ardent passions, the love of liberty and the love of distinction.*
>
> SARAH JOSEPHA HALE, 1835

A growing population

The number of people living in the USA increased from 9.6 million in 1800 to 23 million in 1850 and 63 million by 1890. Some of this population growth came from natural increase. American families were often large, with six or more children. But most of it was due to immigration. Millions of men, women and children made the long, sometimes dangerous, voyage across the Atlantic Ocean. They hoped to escape from hunger or religious persecution, or to make their fortunes in a new land.

Linking east and west

New cities such as Chicago (mid-west) and San Francisco (on the Pacific Ocean coast), also grew rapidly in the 1800s. They were linked to the east coast by new wagon trails, stagecoach routes, railroads and canals. In 1869 the transcontinental railroad, linking New York and California, was completed. By 1890 the USA had one third of the world's railroad tracks. By the end of the century the whole of the USA was linked in one vast and very profitable network of trade.

Westward ho!

In 1803 the US government gained vast new territories, west of the Mississippi River, that had earlier been ruled by France. Later on, in the 1840s, the USA gained yet more land, in Mexico, Florida and the far west. These new possessions sparked off a mass movement of settlers. They left houses and families in the north-eastern states and moved west, to create small prairie homesteads, sprawling cattle ranches and huge grain-growing farms.

Immigrants newly arrived in the United States. From the 1850s to the 1880s immigrants came mostly from Ireland, Germany and Scandinavia. Workers from China and South-east Asia also settled on the west coast of the USA. Between 1880 and 1900 most immigrants came from Russia, Italy and Eastern Europe.

New factories and cities

American businessmen were also keen to build new factories and make use of newly-invented machines. The cloth-making industry, which used fine-quality cotton grown in southern states, was the first to be mechanized. New machinery also changed working habits in steelworks, printworks, potteries, shoe workshops, iron foundries and coal mines. Many big new cities grew up close to factories, rail depots and ports.

Riches underground

American industry received a great boost when two very valuable raw materials – oil and gold – were discovered. In 1848, after gold was found in California, there was a wild gold-rush as people hurried west to lay claim to plots of land. The first oil well in America was up and working by 1859. Oil soon provided cheap fuel for American factories and homes.

This painting shows the bustling city of New York in 1870. New York was a city of contrasts. The business district was full of smart houses, offices and shops. Most people lived on the edges of the city where factories belched out unhealthy smoke.

Cattle waiting to be loaded at a western railyard. Canals and railways carried western farm produce, such as meat, corn and animal skins, to food shops and processing factories in the east.

Setting the scene: USA 1800–1900

1800   1810   1820   1830   1840

GOVERNMENT AND INTERNATIONAL RELATIONS

1800 Washington DC becomes new Federal capital.

1812–1814 War between Britain and USA. In 1814 Britain burns Washington DC.

1818 Borders agreed between USA and Canada.

1823 Monroe Doctrine bans all future colonial settlements on American continent by European powers.

1832 Democratic Party founded.

1836 Battle of the Alamo, in which Texans fight against the USA.

1846–1848 War between Mexico and the USA.

SOCIAL CHANGE

1808 The USA bans import of slaves from Africa.

1820–1840s Mass temperance and anti-slavery campaigns.

1831 Slave revolt in Virginia.

EXPANSION AND SETTLEMENT

1803 Louisiana Purchase: the USA buys vast areas of land from France, and doubles in size.

1804–1808 Lewis and Clark explore western America and reach the west coast.

1820 The USA now has 23 states.

1830s Indian Removal Act: Native American peoples are moved to make room for settlers.

1848 The USA gains California, Nevada, Utah and Colorado.

1848–1849 Californian Gold Rush: people move west in search of gold.

INVENTIONS AND DISCOVERIES

1807 Robert Fulton tests first practical steamboat, the *Clermont*, off New York.

1809 First vehicle-carrying suspension bridge across Merrimack River, Massachusetts.

1819 The first steamship crosses the Atlantic.

1824 Erie Canal, New York, completed.

1828 First railroad in the USA completed (between Baltimore and Ohio).

1831 *The New York Sun*, the first cheap daily paper, launched.

1844 First Morse telegraph system installed between Baltimore and Washington.

1861–1865 The American Civil War.

1870 The 15th Amendment is passed. Voting rights cannot be denied because of race, colour or former slave status.

1865 The 13th Amendment is passed. Slavery is abolished throughout the USA.

1893 Hawaii becomes protectorate of the USA.

1898 Spanish–American War for control of Cuba and the Philippines.

1854 The Republican Party is founded.

1865 Abraham Lincoln is assassinated.

1850 Congress votes for the Compromise of 1850: a law that increases punishments for runaway slaves and people who help them.

1863 Abraham Lincoln issues Emancipation Proclamation: frees slaves in all Confederate (southern) states still in rebellion.

1866 White racist organization Ku Klux Klan founded.

1857 Dred Scott Case: US Supreme Court rules that a slave is not a citizen.

1869 Knights of Labor, a national trade union, is founded.

1880–1900 Golden age for big business, but growing gap between rich and poor.

1853 Gadsden Purchase: the USA gains New Mexico and Arizona.

1860s–1870s Wars for the West: battles between Native Americans and settlers.

1890 The USA has 44 states.

1860 The USA has 33 states.

1870s–1890s More than 130 000 miles of railroads are built to open up the West to settlement and trade.

1862 Homestead Act: encourages settlers to move west by offering 285 million acres of free land.

1867 The USA purchases Alaska from Russia.

1890 Battle of Wounded Knee: last major fight between Native Americans and settlers.

1851 Isaac Singer patents the sewing machine.

1874 First electric train, New York.

1880 Hiram Maxim invents machine gun.

1851 Elisha Otis invents the lift.

1866 First successful underwater telegraph cable between Europe and the USA.

1879 Thomas Edison invents the light bulb.

1890s The USA becomes world's top agricultural producer.

1853 The Colt revolver revolutionizes firearms.

1869 Transcontinental railway completed.

1878 First commercial telephone exchange.

1859 First-ever oil well (Pennsylvania).

1876 First telephone invented by Alexander Graham Bell.

From home to factory

In 1800 most Americans lived in small towns or on farms. They ran small businesses, or grew their own food and made many of their own clothes, furnishings and tools. Sometimes they even built their own homes. By 1900 more than half the population lived in industrial cities and towns, rented rooms, and worked for other people, for wages. In this chapter we look at how this major change in American lifestyle affected women and girls.

Working together

Before 1800 most women worked at home. Women's work involved many separate tasks, such as cooking, cleaning, caring for children, and helping husbands or fathers run family businesses or farms. Ordinary women did all sorts of hard physical labour, such as scrubbing floors, milking cows or cutting corn at harvest time. Rich women had servants (or in southern USA, slaves) to do this work for them, but they often had to take responsibility as household or farm supervisors. Most women were not paid for this work. Instead they were seen as junior partners in the shared family enterprise.

Women carrying out their traditional tasks. This picture was painted in 1870. By this date, only middle-class and upper-class women could afford to stay at home. Many ordinary women had to go out to work to help feed and clothe their families.

A woman shop assistant in Macy's, New York, around 1890. Shops sold luxury items, factory-made goods, ready-prepared foods and useful things, such as soap and candles, that wage-earning women no longer had time to make themselves. Male shop owners hoped that pretty female shop assistants would encourage sales.

Outside the home

Soon after 1800 ordinary women's pattern of working began to change. They began to work outside the home for wages in factories and shops. Factory owners liked employing women. Their fingers were quick and nimble, and they were easier to manage than men. Although most factory owners were male, many other men (and some women) complained when women went out to work. They said that a woman's place was in the home, caring for her husband and children. In fact many wage-earning women also had to look after their homes and families after a long day's work in a factory or shop. The idea of women as 'ladies', civilizing society by their gentle, domestic ways, also became stronger at this time. As wealthy men began to earn money in businesses outside the home, they left behind wives, no longer partners, who were economically dependent.

Factory life

The first factories were built in New England in the 1820s and 1830s. They used machines such as the spinning jenny and the power loom to spin thread and weave cloth – both traditional female tasks. The first factory hands were young, unmarried women and girls, mostly farmers' daughters, who lived in boarding houses next to the factories. Factory work gave them the chance to save for their future as farmers' wives, and proved that women could work as well as men. The first factories paid good wages, because skilled workers were in short supply. Before long widows, deserted wives and married women went to work in factories as well. They hoped to earn money to help themselves or their children to survive.

Women factory-hands operating weaving looms in the 1850s. Machines in factories made goods, like clothes, that women used to make by hand for their families at home.

Women trade union members at the 1886 meeting of the Knights of Labor. In 1887 the Knights of Labor asked Leonora Barry, as women's officer, to advise women union members and collect facts and figures about women and work – the first time this had been done on a nationwide scale.

'Progress' and growing industry

As the American population grew and the economy expanded, more factories were built. Women worked mostly in the food-processing, clothing, footwear, cigar-making and printing trades. Factory work was boring, tiring, unhealthy and increasingly badly paid. As more workers became available, pay rates dropped. Whenever profits fell, factory owners cut women's wages, regardless of how hard they worked. Shifts were long – up to 13 hours a day, and supervisors were strict. Workers who 'misbehaved', even during their time off, lost their jobs.

The first protests

Factory towns became dirty and crowded, working conditions became hotter and noisier, and machines grew faster and more dangerous to operate. As a result, women joined together to protest about pay and work conditions. They staged walkouts and marches to complain about punishments for being late for work. The first walk-out by women was in 1828, from a cotton mill in Dover, New Hampshire.

Trade unions

The first small, local trade unions for women were organized in the 1830s, in New York. In 1845 cloth-factory workers at Lowell, Massachusetts, set up the Female Labor Reform Association. Factory owners did all they could to shame union leaders, and threatened protesters with dismissal, but soon more female unions were formed. These early unions had little success, because union members knew there were plenty of new workers ready to replace them.

Immigrant workers

Newly-arrived immigrants were often desperate to find a job, however badly paid. In the early 1840s most factory workers were American-born. By the 1850s most were immigrants. Factory owners also employed immigrant women to do piecework in sweatshops or at home. Although women trade unionists like Leonora Barry tried to help these workers, immigrant women were often frightened of losing work by protesting, unable to speak much English, and difficult to contact and organize.

Poor families in a crowded New York courtyard, 1870. Each family lived in a single damp, decaying room. The women and children are working together, sorting bundles of filthy rags for sale to scrap merchants and paper makers.

Piecework meant working long hours, sometimes all night, sewing parts of clothes or shoes for a miserably small sum. Women working at home had to pay for their own heat, light and thread.

Little help from men

Male trade unions did not help women workers, because they feared that low-paid women might compete with them for jobs. (Women were usually paid only one half or one third as much as men.) Male unions also did not value women's work equally with their own. In the 1870s and 1880s, one powerful union, the Knights of Labor, began to help women workers fight for their rights. But the Knights collapsed because of quarrels among themselves. The American Federation of Labor, which replaced it, gave working women much less support.

Women speak out

The many rapid changes that took place during the century raised questions about how society should be run. American men could make decisions about their country's future by serving in national and local government, holding public office, and voting for new laws. But women were not allowed to do any of these things.

Voluntary action

Women took action by forming voluntary associations and campaigning groups. They wrote letters, drew up petitions, leaflets and pamphlets, collected money, held meetings and, eventually, began to speak in public. All this took a special kind of courage, because in the early 1800s 'ladylike' women were not supposed to play a part in public life. Instead, they were supposed to make their views known, gently and quietly, by talking to their husbands or male family friends. But gradually women did begin to speak out. They focused their campaigns on four main areas: anti-slavery, religion, welfare and alcohol abuse.

The Great Awakening

From the 1790s to the 1840s powerful Christian preachers in the United States led a religious campaign, called the Second Great Awakening. Many people were moved by the preachers and became convinced that God had saved their souls. Although men led the movement, it appealed especially to women, and gave them the chance to play a new, much more active, part in religious life. They set up Sunday schools and female missionary societies, organized Bible readings and prayer circles, and met other women at religious discussion groups.

Women leading a Quaker Meeting in Philadelphia. In 1800 the Quakers were the only religious group to allow women leaders. Quaker women were very active in trying to abolish slavery, and ran many welfare schemes.

A mother, her children and all her belongings, out on the streets. Women might be made homeless if their husbands fell ill, lost their jobs, or left them. All through the 1800s voluntary workers provided help for women and children in need.

Welfare work

Religious and moral beliefs led wealthy and middle-class women to help less fortunate people. They set up groups to improve poor mothers' lives and raise standards of child care, and founded homes for orphans. They also founded Moral Reform Societies, which helped women prostitutes, and campaigned for better behaviour by men. Women played an important part in the Temperance Movement, which aimed to stop men drinking too much alcohol. Women and children suffered most when husbands spent their wages on alcohol, or if they became violent when they were drunk.

Challenging tradition

Taking voluntary action gave women from all social classes valuable experience of planning and organizing. It gave them confidence in public speaking and fundraising. It also made them challenge people's beliefs about how women should lead their lives.

THE GRIMKÉ SISTERS

From the 1820s onwards, both men and women campaigned to end slavery in the United States. They formed anti-slavery societies, and sent petitions to Congress demanding a change in the law. They tried to persuade people not to buy goods made by slaves. In the early years of the anti-slavery movement, two young Quaker sisters, Sarah and Angelina Grimké, caused a sensation by going on a public speaking tour (1836–1837). Critics called them unnatural and unwomanly, but they attracted large audiences, and won a great deal of support for the anti-slavery cause. The sisters' protest was especially shocking because they came from a southern slave-owning family, and left home rather than be supported by slave labour. They also made a link between the oppression of slaves and how women were also denied their rights by men.

Sarah Grimké (1792–1873)

Angelina Grimké (1805–1879)

One step further

Most women's rights campaigners saw slaves' freedom and women's rights as part of the same cause – equality for all citizens. In 1840 a group of Americans travelled to Britain for an anti-slavery conference. The group included two women, Lucretia Mott and Elizabeth Cady Stanton. They spent much time together, because they were made to sit behind a curtain during the conference (it was too shocking for women to appear in public with men). They decided that back home they would organize a conference of their own. Its subject would be women's rights.

Seneca Falls

There were some delays, but finally Cady Stanton and Mott managed to put their plan into action. In 1848 more than 200 women (and 40 men) met at Seneca Falls, New York, in the first-ever Women's Rights Convention. They drew up a list of ways in which women were unfairly treated. They called it a Declaration of Sentiments, because they wanted everyone to compare it with the Declaration of Independence, which in 1776 had promised so many rights to American men. In 1850 the first National Women's Rights Convention was held in Massachusetts. It marked the beginning of an organized movement by women all over the United States to win equal civil rights with men.

Lucretia Mott (1793–1880) was a Quaker leader and founder of the Philadelphia Female Anti-slavery Society. Here, in the centre of an angry crowd, she is shown as calm and determined.

> *I believe He (God) gave me longings and yearnings to be filled, and that He did not mean all our time to be devoted to feeding and clothing the body... The widening of women's sphere is to improve her lot. Let us do it, and if the world scoff, let it scoff!*
>
> LUCY STONE, 1855

Opposition

Straight away, the women faced opposition from men, and from women too. But, led by tireless, determined organizers, the women continued with their demands. Then in 1861 their campaigns were interrupted by something more important than hostile opinions – America was at war!

THE DECLARATION OF SENTIMENTS

The Declaration of Sentiments demanded equal rights for women, and claimed that women were treated unfairly because:

1 Women could not vote.
2 Women had to obey laws, but had no say in how they were made.
3 Women had fewer rights than criminals.
4 Women had no representatives to put forward their views in government.
5 When women married they lost all legal rights over their bodies.
6 When women married they lost all legal rights over wages and property.
7 Married women had to obey their husbands, who had the right to beat them and imprison them.
8 Women were not allowed to see their children again if they were divorced.
9 Single women had to pay taxes, but had no say in how the government spent them.
10 Women could not work in well-paid professional jobs. Their wages were always lower than men's.
11 Women could not go to college or university.
12 Women were not allowed to be ministers of religion.
13 If a woman behaved like a man, she became an outcast.
14 Men were playing God by telling women how to lead their lives.
15 Men's attitudes and actions had destroyed women's self-confidence and self-respect, and had made them willing to lead lowly, dependent lives.

A great leader

Two of the most energetic campaigners for women's rights were Elizabeth Cady Stanton (right) and Susan B Anthony (below). They met at an anti-slavery meeting and made friends immediately. Cady Stanton (1815–1902) was warm, out-going and a radical thinker. She studied with her father in his law office, where she saw how unfairly women were treated by the law. She campaigned against slavery. She organized the International Council of Women and led the National Women's Suffrage Association, which called for votes for women. She was a skilled writer and edited the feminist newspaper *The Revolution*. She also managed the household for her husband, and brought up their seven children.

Radical thoughts

Susan B Anthony (1820–1906) was brought up by a Quaker father, who educated her equally with her brothers. When her father lost all his money, she became a teacher. Her first interest in reform was in the temperance movement, but she found that people wouldn't take her seriously because she was a woman.

Cady Stanton began to persuade her friend to help her in campaigning for women's rights. Anthony organized petitions to support the Married Women's Property Act (1860) and campaigned for equal education and women's trade unions. She went on long speaking tours to raise money for *The Revolution,* and campaigned in the States and in Europe for women's right to vote.

Anti-slavery

Women did not have equal rights with men in the new union of states in America. But another group of people had even fewer rights – black men and women slaves. These African-Americans were descended from captives who had been shipped across the Atlantic Ocean to work as servants and labourers. By law, slaves belonged to their owners. They were forced to live on their owner's plantations, and could be beaten or killed if they tried to run away. Women slaves faced special horrors. They had to work in the fields while they were pregnant or soon after giving birth, and were often harassed by white men. Their children might be taken away and sold as slaves.

> *They are our countrywomen, they are our sisters, and to us as women, they have a right to look for sympathy with their sorrows, and effort and prayer for their rescue…*
>
> SARAH GRIMKÉ, WRITING ABOUT WOMEN SLAVES

The fight for freedom
In the 1820s northern states began to outlaw slavery. But states in the south, where most of the sugar and cotton was grown, refused to do the same. In 1833 a national organization called the American Anti-slavery Society was formed in the north to campaign against slavery.

Slaves working on a cotton plantation. Mothers had to leave children and babies by the side of the field. If they stopped to care for them, even if they were crying, the women were punished.

Women start to campaign

A separate women's national anti-slavery movement was set up in 1837. Many women from different backgrounds joined in to help the slaves fight for freedom. They wrote letters, held meetings and raised funds. Some male anti-slavery campaigners were hostile to women who supported their cause. They did not want the anti-slavery issue to become linked to women's own demands. But other men, such as the newspaper editor and ex-slave Frederick Douglass, welcomed women's help. Looking back on the struggle, Douglass wrote, 'When the true history of the anti-slavery cause shall be written, women will occupy a large space in its pages, for the cause of the slave has been peculiarly a women's cause.' In return for their support some men who fought against slavery began to campaign for women's rights too.

Harriet Tubman (far left) worked for the Underground Railroad. After the abolition of slavery she continued to speak out for the rights of women and all black people.

Sojourner Truth

Two of the most courageous women who fought to end slavery were Sojourner Truth and Harriet Tubman, both former slaves. Sojourner Truth was born in 1777 in New York State, and escaped in 1827, the year before slavery was abolished there. She worked as a servant, then travelled the country, speaking out against slavery and in support of women's rights. She was a tall, impressive woman, and a magical speaker. Even hostile men listened to her passionate words and powerful arguments.

Sojourner Truth, photographed around 1815.

Harriet Tubman

Harriet Tubman was born in 1820 in Maryland, where slavery was still allowed. She risked her life by running away and escaping to the north, dressed as a workman. There she helped to organize a network of secret trackways and overnight hiding places called the Underground Railroad, so that other slaves could also run away. She rescued her parents and her brothers, and led many others to safety. Between 1830 and 1860 the Underground Railroad helped about 50 000 slaves to escape to freedom.

Women and war

In 1860 northerner Abraham Lincoln, who opposed slavery, was elected president. As a result, the state of South Carolina decided to leave the United States, soon followed by ten more southern states. There were many disagreements between the north and south, such as how much freedom states should have to make their own laws. There were economic and cultural rivalries too – but slavery aroused the strongest feelings on both sides.

In wartime women took on many jobs that used to be done only by men. These women are filling cartridges with gunpowder at the Union army's weapons factory.

War begins

There was so much anger that in 1861 a Civil War broke out between the north (known as the Union) and the south (called the Confederacy). It lasted until 1865, when the south surrendered. In the same year Lincoln's government passed the 13th Amendment to the Constitution, making slavery illegal throughout the United States.

Fighting for a cause

Although women were not allowed to join the army, many women played an important part in the war, on both sides. Women writers wrote pamphlets, explaining their side's views. A few daring women disguised themselves as men so they could join the fighting. Other women risked their lives by carrying messages, or by acting as lookouts and spies. Rose Greenhow spied for the Confederate side. She was arrested while trying to swallow a message written in secret code. Northerner Pauline Cushman pretended to make friends with a Confederate engineer and stole all the plans of his forts.

Belle Boyd was a Confederate spy. She smuggled guns and ammunition across the border to armies in the south.

Dorothea Lynde Dix (1802–1887) set high standards of nursing care. She preferred nurses to be over 30, and simply dressed in brown or black clothes, with no jewellery.

Medical care

In peacetime women were used to nursing sick and injured members of their own families, so it seemed natural for them to care for soldiers injured in war. Battle commanders welcomed the thousands of women who volunteered to serve as army nurses, but were surprised when Dorothea Dix was put in charge of all nursing services for the Union army. Dix was just one of many women who proved how useful they could be in wartime. Pioneer doctor Elizabeth Blackwell set up the Ladies' Central Relief Committee to provide medical treatment for soldiers. Some women turned their houses into hospitals. Clara Barton set up a bureau to help families find dead or injured relations.

Women left their families to work as nurses during the Civil War. Conditions on battlefields and in hospitals were grim. One nurse wrote that, 'we have to kneel in blood and water, but we think nothing of it at all'.

Women alone

While men were away fighting, women had to take over their jobs. They ran family businesses and farms, and worked in government offices, schools and factories. Some ran workshops of their own. Katherine Prescott Wormley won a contract to make army uniforms. She employed mostly soldiers' wives, who had no income while their husbands were away. Inventor Martha Costan developed a signal flare, used by warships at sea, that saved many sailors' lives.

Women's reward

All through the war women showed that they could be just as brave, hard-working and responsible as men. But this did not change the way many men thought about women's place in society, or encourage the government to give women the rights they claimed. Once the war was over, women campaigners took up the struggle once more.

A citizen's rights

After slavery was abolished in 1865, women turned all their energies to fighting their own cause. Although by that time they had won several rights and freedoms, they still did not have the right to serve on a jury, to run for public office, or to vote. Because of this, many women felt that they were being treated as second-class citizens.

> The day will come when man will recognize woman as his peer, not only at the fireside but in the counsels of the nation. Then, not until then, will there be the perfect comradeship, the ideal union between the sexes...
>
> SUSAN B ANTHONY, 1897

Not equal to men

In 1868, three years after the Civil War ended, the government added the 14th Amendment to the Constitution. It aimed to give all US citizens 'equal protection of the laws', and to stop southern states denying former slaves the right to vote. But, for the first time, voters were defined as males living in the USA. It seemed as if Congress was trying to make it more difficult for women to get the vote. In 1870 the 15th Amendment guaranteed equal rights to all voters, regardless of race or colour, but made no mention of women at all. The government was still refusing to give women, black or white, the same rights as men.

Which way forward?

Women's rights leaders discussed how they should continue their campaign. Some, like Elizabeth Cady Stanton, believed they should refuse to support the government's plan to give the vote to black men until women got the vote too. Others, like Lucy Stone, believed that once black men had the vote, it would soon be extended to women. As a result of these disagreements, two separate national organizations were set up in 1869 to fight for women's rights.

Women giving evidence to a Senate committee, 1871. Congress appointed committees to discuss women's rights to vote, but dismissed the debate as ridiculous in 1887.

From 1868 women organized voting demonstrations. They attended elections and cast votes, even though this was illegal.

A split amongst the campaigners

The National Woman Suffrage Association was led by Elizabeth Cady Stanton and Susan B Anthony. It fought at a national level on a range of women's rights issues. It published a newspaper, called *The Revolution*, which discussed (for that time) shocking issues such as divorce and prostitution. It had the slogan, 'Men, their rights and nothing more; women, their rights and nothing less.' The more moderate American Woman Suffrage Association was founded by Lucy Stone. It focused on voting rights alone, and worked at a local level, trying to persuade each state in turn to give women the vote. For members of both organizations, a long struggle lay ahead.

Marriage and careers

As well as continuing their fight for the vote, women also campaigned for changes to the unfair laws and customs governing other important areas of their lives, including marriage, education and careers. You can read about these on the following pages.

FIGHTING FOR EQUALITY

Lucy Stone (1818–1893) was a farmer's daughter. Although her father opposed her, she managed to save up enough money from teaching to attend Oberlin College. She travelled long distances to make speeches and organize rallies for the Anti-slavery Society, and soon began to speak on women's issues too. In 1855 she married Henry Blackwell, a reformer who supported women's rights. From 1866 she spent her life campaigning for the vote. She collapsed while still working, aged 75, and her daughter Alice Stone Blackwell continued her campaigns into the twentieth century.

Marriage partners

Legally, American girls came of age when they were 18 years old. They could marry without their parents' permission, and while they stayed single could keep any property they owned, including their wages. But they lost these rights when they married, and had very few others.

> *The present laws of marriage ... refuse to recognize the wife as an independent, rational being, while they confer on the husband an injurious and unnatural superiority...*
>
> LUCY STONE AND HENRY BLACKWELL, 1855

Equal partners

Most women wanted to get married and have children. They believed that happy families were the basis of a well-run society. Yet even though they supported the idea of marriage, many women campaigned for marriage reform. They wanted wives to have equal rights with husbands, recognition for their work as homemakers, and the chance of an independent role outside marriage as well.

Married names

Feminist campaigners believed that names were signs of personal identity. Boys carried on a family surname from generation to generation, but girls were expected to change their names completely when they married. Women's rights campaigners objected to this. In 1878 Elizabeth Cady Stanton explained to a friend: 'The custom of calling women Mrs John This and Mrs Tom That ... is founded on the principle that white men are lords of all.'

This picture was painted in 1868. It shows a traditional middle-class family. Many men said that marriage reform would destroy family life. But women campaigners believed that equal marriages would work better than unequal ones.

Property rights

In 1830 Ernestine L Rose (see page 44) began a long campaign for women's right to own their own property and wages once they were married. She spent 12 years collecting signatures and presenting petitions to Congress. In 1848 New York State passed a law allowing divorced women to keep the goods they owned before marriage. It also stopped a wife being held responsible for her husband's debts. But wives still had no right to keep their own earnings and no right to the custody of their children.

Continuing the campaign

Susan B Anthony (see page 17) decided to join Rose's campaign. She organized a team of 60 women to seek public support and lobby Congress. Finally, in 1860, New York State made a law giving married women rights to all their property, to their wages, to the guardianship of their children, and to inherit their dead husband's property. Many other northern and western states followed New York's example.

An American bride on her wedding day, around 1850. Was this the happiest day of her life – or the end of her legal freedom?

Unfair divorce

Women also protested about unfair laws on divorce. Each state had its own laws, but these usually meant that a woman who parted from her husband had to leave her home, and had no right to any financial support. Often she became a social outcast too. In 1860 Elizabeth Cady Stanton drew up a list of ten reasons why divorce should be discussed at the National Women's Rights Convention. Many people were so shocked that the subject was dropped from the agenda. Even so, women did leave unhappy marriages, and by the late 1800s the USA had the highest divorce rate in the world.

Women were responsible for bringing up children. Many women told their children stories of their struggles for rights and freedom. They hoped their daughters' lives would be better than their own.

Wages for housework?

Some campaigners turned their attention to women's traditional role as homemaker. Caring for home and family was skilful work. But when campaigners such as Sarah Josepha Hale argued that women's work at home should be paid like any other profession, they were laughed at. Charlotte Perkins Gilman put forward even more radical views. She said that society would be better if men and women were both free to go out to work, and if families hired cleaners, bought their meals in neighbourhood canteens, and paid day nurseries to care for their children.

Married bodies

The law said that wives could not own their own property. It also said that a wife's body belonged to her husband. This, together with custom and public opinion, helped to restrict women's rights over their health and their appearance in many ways. Women were usually kept in ignorance about how their bodies worked. Public opinion believed that girls should be innocent, and that no respectable woman would discuss sex or human biology, even with her husband or closest female friends. As a result many women suffered years of pain or illness, because they were too ignorant or embarrassed to seek medical help.

Too many children

Women also suffered and died from giving birth to large families of children. Despite this, giving advice on family planning was illegal. Abortion was also illegal, but many poor women took dangerous mixtures of herbs and drugs to try and end their pregnancies, since they felt unable to feed or look after another child. Even by the early 1900s the situation was little better. Margaret Sanger (1883–1966), a pioneering doctor who created the term family planning, went abroad to study because she could not find the information she needed in the USA. When she opened a family planning clinic in Brooklyn in 1916, she was arrested for causing a public nuisance.

Charlotte Perkins Gilman (1860–1935) was a socialist and feminist writer who wanted to end the idea that there was men's work and women's work.

Unhealthy fashions from a popular women's magazine, round about 1880.

Unhealthy fashions

Campaigners such as Amelia Jenks Bloomer, editor of one of America's first women's magazines, *The Lily*, argued against fashions that dangerously changed women's natural shape. Between 1825 and 1875 wide skirts were fashionable. Some were made from more than 20 metres of cloth. They weighed so much that a padded frame had to be worn underneath. Tight corsets were also popular, and girls pulled the laces as tight as they could to make their waist as slim as possible. Both styles were unhealthy. Heavy skirts caused backache and were a fire risk. Tight corsets caused indigestion and liver disease.

Bloomers

In the 1850s Bloomer led a campaign for dress reform. She called for women's clothes to be healthy, practical and comfortable, rather than just pretty. Bloomer and her colleagues wore loose corsets and short, full skirts over baggy trousers. These soon became known as bloomers. Some dress reformers also wore copies of men's clothing. All these women were laughed at in the streets.

This costume, popular among feminists, was first worn in public at the Seneca Falls Convention in 1848.

Marriage and appearance

Society expected women to spend plenty of time on their appearance, and to judge themselves and other women by how attractive they were to men. The wives of wealthy men were often encouraged to wear expensive clothes and jewels, to advertise their husband's success. This meant that plain, badly-dressed or elderly women often felt worthless and rejected. Many women liked nice clothes, and found them a boost to their self-confidence. But feminists complained that too much time thinking about clothes stopped women thinking about other, more important, things.

Right to learn

Until the nineteenth century boys were better educated than girls. This was because people believed that boys should be prepared for an active, decision-making role in society. Women campaigners realized that a good education was essential if girls wanted to lead interesting lives, or follow well-paid careers, without having to depend on men.

> When, with my brothers, I reached forth after the sources of knowledge, I was reproved with, 'It isn't fit for you; it doesn't belong to women.'
>
> LUCY STONE, 1855

Girls and boys were usually taught different subjects. This photograph was taken in 1900, showing that, even at the end of the century, many women were still expected to learn traditional female sewing and housecraft skills.

Opportunities and privileges

People believed that boys' minds were better suited to study. Education gave boys many opportunities that were not open to girls. It prepared them for professional careers, such as engineering, medicine or law, or a life of public speaking and public service as ministers of religion or as politicians. Boys from wealthy families were sent away to school, where they studied subjects such as science, philosophy and Latin. Poorer boys might only go to the local school, but they almost all had the chance to be trained in farmwork, business or craft skills.

Not for girls

Most people believed that girls did not need an academic education. Their future was in the home, as helpers of men. Too much study might even be bad for their health. There were a few private schools for wealthy girls, but they were very expensive and often badly run. They taught reading, writing and simple maths, along with 'feminine' subjects, such as music, needlework and art. Many free primary schools, run by local communities, did not admit girls at all.

Emma Willard (1787–1870) believed that the whole nation would benefit if women were better educated.

New schools

Soon after 1800, women campaigners began to demand better education for girls. Some women, such as Emma Hart Willard, opened their own schools where girls could study 'male' subjects, such as philosophy and maths. But money to run these new schools was hard to find. Teachers often had to spend time fundraising as well as teaching long hours in school. In 1819 Willard drew up a Plan for Improving Female Education and sent copies to the governor of New York State. In it, she asked for the state to pay towards the cost of education. In 1821 the town council at Troy, New York, became the first council to give state help for a girls' secondary school.

TEACHERS

Many well-educated women trained to be teachers at school and, towards the end of the century, at college. Some set up and managed their own schools. Schoolteaching was one of the few 'respectable' occupations for women. By the 1870s most teachers were women. Many women felt they had a duty to help girls develop their minds, fulfil their ambitions and escape from a life of housework or boring, badly-paid jobs. Black teachers such as Fanny Jackson Coppin, a former slave, aimed to educate freed black men and women, so they could play an important part in American society after the Civil War.

A woman teaching physics to college girls at the end of the century.

After school and college

By 1850 most American girls went to primary school and could read and write. Thanks to campaigners, many new secondary schools for girls were opened from the 1820s onwards. Some were privately-run, others were helped by charities or state funds. But women could not hope for a well-paid, professional career unless they graduated from college or university.

> When women can support themselves, have their entry to all the trades and professions, with a house of their own over their heads and a bank account, they will own their bodies and be dictators [rulers] in the social realm.
>
> ELIZABETH CADY STANTON, DIARY ENTRY 1890.

The first four

In 1837 Oberlin College, Ohio, a men's college, allowed the first four female college students to enrol. Oberlin also welcomed black students, a big step towards equality at that time. But none of the women students, black or white, could join in all the men's lessons, and they had to help clean the male students' rooms, serve their meals and wash their clothes.

For women only

The first women-only college in America was founded at Mount Holyoke by Mary Lyon, in 1837. Students could study subjects such as botany, chemistry, geography, history, and logic. In the first term 80 pupils enrolled. By the next year the college had become so popular that more than 400 applicants had to be turned away. Soon other women's colleges opened. In 1855 the University of Iowa was the first mixed university, admitting women and men on equal terms.

WELLESLEY COLLEGE

BY MISS GOODLOE

ILLUSTRATED IN THE

MAY SCRIBNER'S

This magazine cover from 1897 shows students at Wellesley College, Massachusetts. It was founded in 1880 to provide university education for young women.

Emma Nutt became the world's first telephone operator in 1878. By 1890 there were more than a quarter of a million telephones in the USA, and thousands of women worked as operators.

Professions

Once women began to receive a better education, they wanted to enter traditionally male professions, such as law and the civil service. Such jobs were challenging and well-paid. But women found that many men did not want them to train for these careers. Belva Lockwood, who won fame as a lawyer, was at first rejected by many law schools because she was female. She fought on and built up a large legal practice. Lockwood won a famous law case against the government for Cherokee Native peoples' rights. She was also an active campaigner for women's right to vote, for equal pay, for black people and immigrants, and for international peace.

Office careers

Towards the end of the nineteenth century, new inventions opened up new careers for women, as secretaries and clerks. Typewriters were invented in the 1860s, and soon became essential in most businesses, offices and law-courts. In 1877 the New York YMCA offered the world's first typing course, exclusively for women. In the same year, the world's first telephone switchboard was installed in Boston.

A network of support

In 1868 Elizabeth Cady Stanton founded the Working Women's Association, to encourage women to join the professions, and to provide support. It also helped many women in factories, offices and shops to fight for equal treatment with men. New magazines, written by women, also helped publicize topics of importance to professional women, as well as providing careers for women journalists, editors and printers.

Women clerks leaving work at the Treasury Department building in Washington DC, 1865.

Medicine, nursing and welfare work

Many women were capable nurses, relying mainly on common sense. But few had knowledge of new medical techniques. This was because nursing was seen as one of women's traditional roles, and not as a profession. The first three nursing schools were not set up until after the Civil War, in 1873. A professional association for nurses was finally founded in 1896.

Medical study

Medicine was a 'male' subject. Long before the Civil War women began to demand the right to go to medical school. But they faced prejudice from doctors and students, who said that women were not clever or strong enough to study medicine. They claimed that it was not right for women to go to lectures and examine bodies alongside men.

Some of the first professionally-trained nurses (in white caps) helping doctors with an operation, in the 1870s.

Training for women

Pioneer Harriot Kezia Hunt, who opened a medical clinic for women and children in Boston in 1834, learned as much as she could by studying with helpful local doctors. But Elizabeth Blackwell wanted a proper medical training. The other students refused to speak to her, but she became the first woman to graduate from a US medical school, in 1849. Upset by Blackwell's experiences, a group of rich Quaker women set up the first Female Medical College, in Pennsylvania, in 1850. Others soon followed. For many years, women doctors and medical students faced opposition from men, but by 1890, in some big cities such as Boston, almost one fifth of the doctors were women.

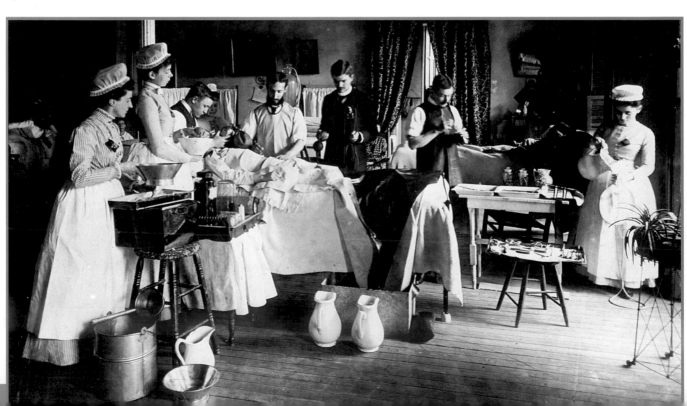

Women medical students watching women doctors perform an operation in a newly-built operating theatre, in the late 1890s.

Research

Women scientists such as Dorothea Dix and Mary Putnam Jacobi also campaigned for better mental health care and for more attention to be given to women's diseases. Others carried out valuable medical research. In 1891 Anna Wessel Williams discovered a powerful natural chemical that could be used to protect children against a deadly disease called diptheria. Over the years, it has saved millions of lives all round the world.

Elizabeth Blackwell (1821–1910) was the first woman to qualify as a doctor in the USA. When she found that male-run hospitals would not employ her, she opened her own hospital, the New York Infirmary for Women and Children, in 1857.

WELFARE WORK

Towards the end of the 1800s poverty and unemployment grew worse in the USA, especially in big cities. In their traditional role as carers women had always been expected to help others. But now women pioneers campaigned for real changes. In 1874 Etta Angel Wheeler founded the American Society for the Prevention of Cruelty to Children, after she found a little girl wandering naked, beaten and half-starved in the streets of New York. Pioneer welfare workers such as Jane Addams and Mary McDowell opened advice and aid centres in New York and Chicago. Other campaigning women set up consumers unions, to tell the public about employers who paid low wages and mistreated their workers, and to ask them not to buy their goods.

FRONTIER EXPERIENCE

Settling new land

From the 1840s to the 1880s, large numbers of families made the dangerous journey from eastern America to uncharted territory west of the Mississippi River. They believed they had a God-given right to make a new life for themselves in frontier lands. The US government encouraged this movement by driving the original Native American inhabitants from their homelands, and by passing laws that gave settlers free land.

It was not an unusual thing to meet a woman coming from the fields where she had been hoeing cotton, with a small bucket or cup on her head, and a hoe over her shoulder, smoking a pipe and briskly knitting as she strode along. I have seen, added to all these, a baby strapped to her back.

ELIZABETH BOTUME, 1893

A group of pioneers travelling west in midwinter, making camp for the night.

On the trail
Families heading west loaded their belongings on to covered wagons, pulled by horses or oxen. The journey took many months, through scorching heat and bitter winter snows. Finding food and drinking water was a constant problem, as was keeping clean. Many babies were born along the way, and many women and children died.

Hard work
Women settlers' tasks were often physically exhausting. They weeded fields and gardens, tended seedlings, dried grass for hay, dug up vegetables, and helped to harvest crops. They fed and milked the cows, made butter and cheese, reared chickens, collected eggs, preserved fruit and vegetables by bottling or salting, and gathered edible wild berries, nuts and mushrooms. They helped build farmhouses out of timber or slabs of earth, and learned to cope when their homes became infested with insects and snakes.

Patchwork began as a way of recycling pieces from worn-out clothes. But women's sewing skills turned patchwork into an art form. Friends and neighbours often exchanged scraps of cloth, and each quilt became a collection of memories and thoughts.

Self-reliance

In remote areas, women had to be very self-reliant. They taught their children, arranged prayer meetings, and nursed sick people and animals. They might also have to shoot wild animals that attacked their homesteads, or defend their farms from outlaws and Native Americans. They lived in constant anxiety. If tornadoes flattened their crops, or if summer heat and drought killed their animals, they and their families might die.

Community life

Women travelling west gave one another companionship, sympathy and support. If they lived in villages they had the chance of a lively community life. There were shared projects like quilting bees (sewing evenings), village dances, and regular annual celebrations such as harvest home. But life on remote farms could be lonely without friends and relations living nearby.

Women farming pioneers

Frontier farming was a risky business, and farmers' wives were often left to manage alone after their husbands died. Some women pioneers were very successful. They not only carried on their husband's farm business, but expanded it as well. In 1884 a widow called Harriet W R Strong planted walnut trees in California, and experimented with dams, sluices and other water systems to make sure her trees stayed alive. Her ideas were copied in many parts of America. In 1886 Henrietta Moorse King inherited 600 000 acres of land in Texas when her husband died. She and her daughter encouraged the railroad company to build tracks near her farm to carry cattle to market, invested in new technology for drilling wells, and bred a new strain of cow.

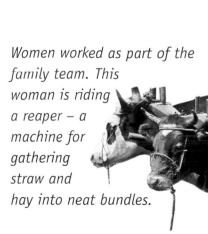

Women worked as part of the family team. This woman is riding a reaper – a machine for gathering straw and hay into neat bundles.

New roles and opportunities

Life in the frontier lands was often hard and sometimes dangerous, but it offered women the chance to start new lives away from the strict social customs of long-established villages and towns.

Business schemes

Because frontier farming was so unreliable, women often tried to earn extra money to make ends meet. Some ran boarding houses for travellers, or cooked evening meals for single men. Some enterprising women, like Ma Pullen, who cooked for hungry gold prospectors in Alaska, used their cooking skills to run successful catering businesses. Other women spun cloth, and sewed shirts and trousers for sale. In towns they found jobs as waitresses, washerwomen, cooks and cleaners. Black women worked as servants and nursemaids in the richer settlers' homes. Some women became barmaids and entertainers, although people thought they were not respectable. Educated women ran schools, or wrote adventure novels and columns for newspapers, describing life on the wild frontier.

Annie Oakley was a frontier woman, and an expert shot with a gun. As a girl, she earned enough money to pay off her family's debts by shooting and selling game. When she was only 15 years old she married her husband after beating him in a public shooting match. She made her living by giving shooting displays in circuses and 'Wild West' shows.

Civilization?

Many women also felt that it was their role to civilize the wild frontier lands. They organized prayer meetings and women's clubs, and raised funds for new church buildings or to start local libraries and schools. They held tea parties, and ran reading clubs and music societies. They organized collections for welfare and missionary schemes. Like women in the eastern states, they campaigned for causes they believed in, such as temperance, women's rights, the abolition of slavery and the fight against gambling and violence.

Women first voted in Wyoming in 1869. Onlookers said that there were none of the usual riots and drunken fights, but that 'It was more like a Sunday than a voting day'.

Still not equal

There were many opportunities for women in the west. In most states, they were allowed to own plots of land, and some became successful farm managers. By 1890 a quarter of a million women were running their own ranches or farms. Women were also allowed greater social freedom, because it was simply not always possible to follow traditional customs – such as only leaving the house in the company of a female companion. Some women also enjoyed the freedom to take part in adventurous outdoor sports, such as horse-riding and shooting. Everywhere women were valued because in frontier states there were far fewer women than men. But even though everyone admired frontier women's courage and energy, they still did not have equal freedom with men, or equal civil rights.

Better rights

Frontier women's rights were better than those for women in other parts of the USA. Most frontier states gave married women rights to hold property, to keep their own earnings, and to arrange a fairly equal divorce settlement. In many states, male and female teachers and other government employees earned equal pay.

The vote – at last!

Even more important, the only four states to give women the vote before 1900 (Wyoming in 1869, Utah in 1870, Colorado in 1890, and Idaho in 1890) were in the West. Mostly, this happened for local reasons, not because frontier men were more advanced thinkers. For example, in 1869 Esther Morris, a feminist campaigner, persuaded the governor of Wyoming that women had an important part to play in civilizing lawless male settlers. She told him that women would work hard to improve law and order if he allowed them to serve on juries and gave them the vote. To show they meant business, the first female jurors in Wyoming tried every single bar-keeper in the state capital for breaking Sunday-drinking laws.

SUMMING UP THE CENTURY

The fight continues

Imagine the scene. It is 1892, in Texas. A group of farmhands are drinking in the town's saloon. Suddenly, through the door bursts a middle-aged woman, wielding a hatchet and singing hymns. She is six feet tall and powerfully built, and has soon smashed the bar, and all its bottles, to pieces. This is Carrie Nation, staging the latest raid in her one-woman campaign against drink.

By the end of the century educated American women had achieved greater freedom and confidence to mix socially with men on more equal terms, and to take part in discussions on all the latest newsworthy topics.

Modern inventions have banished the spinning wheel, and the same law of progress makes the woman of today a different woman from her grandmother.

ELIZABETH CADY STANTON, 1881

Public protests

Carrie Nation was eccentric. Few other women behaved like her. But her protests would have been unthinkable at the beginning of the century. In many ways, Carrie Nation's behaviour shows how much women's lives had changed. She was a woman, on her own, taking public action for a cause she believed in. Her outburst was part of a series of protests across America, planned, organized and funded by women, without help from men.

A businesswoman in her office. By the end of the 1800s, educated women had won the right to follow professional careers, and to work as equal colleagues with educated men.

Success or failure

Women had changed public opinion about what they could and could not do, through long, hard campaigns. But after a century's campaigning, what had women achieved? Some changes in the law and a gradual change in public opinion. By 1900 women had won the right to own property and keep their earnings. They had better opportunities in their education and careers. But even so, they were still not equal with men. Businesses still refused to give women equal pay with men, and social customs still gave men much greater freedom to do as they chose. Most important of all, nearly all women in the USA still did not have the right to vote.

Many women, many lives

The major changes in American society affected all women's lives. In big cities many working women were still very disadvantaged by unhealthy housing, low wages and limited education. New factories, growing cities, big business, mass immigration, western frontier settlements and an increasing gap between rich and poor all meant that by 1900 there was no such thing as a typical American way of life. Women in 1900 shared many hopes and ambitions, but their lives were no longer the same.

Into the next century

American women continued their fight for the vote into the twentieth century, led by Alice Stone Blackwell (1857–1950), daughter of Lucy Stone. Some suffragists were prepared to take militant action, but most continued to campaign by peaceful means. Women throughout America were finally granted the vote when the 19th Amendment to the US Constitution was passed in 1920.

The president's speech at the annual convention of the New York Suffrage Association, 1888. By working in groups such as this, campaigning women achieved many changes in the way American society was run.

Women's campaigns

1800–1820s
Religious revival movement. Many more women take part than men. They arrange Bible study classes and discussion groups. This gives women experience of organizing, and of discussing society's rights and wrongs.

1810

1810–1830s Start of campaign for better education for girls. In 1819 Emma Hart asks for state aid to set up girls' schools. In 1821, the town council at Troy, NY, votes for first state-aided female school. In 1833 Oberlin, Ohio, is the first college to admit women to study on equal terms with men. In 1833 Prudence Crandall opens the first school for black girls at Canterbury, Conn.

1820

1828–1829 Radical writer Fanny Wright goes on a lecture tour. She calls for freedom of thought, better conditions for workers, and equality for women.

1820s to 1850s
Women campaign against slavery. Many local female anti-slavery societies are set up, where white and black women campaign together. In 1837–1838 the Grimké sisters go on an anti-slavery public speaking tour. The first national women's anti-slavery convention is held in New York, 1837. In 1847 Lucy Stone begins a career of public speaking. She links anti-slavery with women's rights.

1820s–1840s
Women authors write about women's rights. Margaret Fuller edits *The Dial* – a Boston newspaper that encourages men *and* women to fulfil their potential.

1830

1830s Ernestine Rose starts campaign for Married Women's Property Law in New York State. It is passed in 1848, and gives married women control over goods they owned before marriage. Between 1839 and 1850 most other states pass laws giving married women limited property rights.

1830s First women's trade unions formed. The first woman-only factory strike is held in Dover, New Hampshire, in 1834.

1838 Dorothea Dix begins campaign for reform of prisons and mental hospitals, and better nursing care.

1840

1830s–1840s
Harriot Hunt and Elizabeth Blackwell begin campaigns for women to train as doctors and nurses. Blackwell is the first woman to qualify as a doctor, in 1849.

1840s Women's campaigns for temperance gain strength throughout the USA.

1848 First women's rights convention at Seneca Falls.

1849 Amelia Bloomer sets up temperance journal, *The Lily*. It also campaigns for women's rights.

1850

1850 First National Women's Rights Convention, is held at Worcester, Massachusetts. It is the beginning of a nationwide campaign for equal civil rights and the right to vote.

1855 At their wedding, Lucy Stone and Henry Blackwell protest about wives' unequal rights.

1850s–1870s Women settlers in frontier states play a leading part in campaigning for equal rights, and the vote. (They have fewer old laws to overturn than women in the east.)

1860 New York State passes a law giving married women the right to keep all property and wages, to become joint guardian of their children, and inherit their husband's property.

1860s Increasing demands for women's vote. The first women's voting demonstration is held in 1868, in New Jersey. Women attend an election and cast votes, even though this is illegal.

1863–1865 National Women's Loyal League campaigns in support of the 13th Amendment to outlaw slavery.

1867–1868 Many women oppose the 14th Amendment to the Constitution, which gives equal legal rights to all 'males' rather than to all 'citizens'. This loses them some support.

1869 Women's suffrage movement splits. The radical National Woman Suffrage Association campaigns for legal equality, working women's welfare and social change. The more moderate American Woman Suffrage Association campaigns only for women's right to vote.

1874 Frances Willard founds the National Women's Christian Temperance Union. It becomes the largest women's movement in the nation.

1870s–1890s First territories/states give women voting rights – Wyoming (1869) and Utah (1870).

1878 The 'Anthony Amendment' is first introduced to Congress. It aims to give women equality in all legal rights, but is repeatedly rejected. In 1882 Congress appoints committees to discuss women's suffrage, but votes against it in 1887.

1876 Women demanding the vote disrupt Fourth of July celebrations at the new national Independence Hall, Philadelphia.

1880–1890s More women form trade unions. In 1887 the Knights of Labor ask Leonora Barry to collect facts about women and work. But the Knights organization collapses. Many women's unions are weak and penniless. Many women are afraid to join. Male unions fear women will lower all wages.

1890 The two rival women's suffrage organizations unite. Alice Stone Blackwell is leader. Local and national campaigns continue.

1890s Black women's clubs form national organizations: the National Federation of Afro-American Women (1895), the National Association of Colored Women (1896).

1890 New York Consumers League is founded. It aims to shame bad employers and increase public demand for proper treatment of workers. By the early 1900s this has led to demands for laws to protect women workers, and to a stronger women's trade union movement.

1850

1860

1870

1880

1890

1900

FAME IN A MAN'S WORLD

Before 1800 the world outside the home was mostly a man's world. But during the nineteenth century, because of better education and changing social attitudes, more women than ever before began to work in a variety of careers. Even so, women needed good luck and determination to make their way. On the next four pages, you can read about some of the women who were successful in their chosen careers, and won fame in a man's world. You can also read about a few outstanding women who attracted praise, and sometimes blame, in other ways.

Maria Mitchell (1818–1889)

Mitchell (right) was educated by her father and helped him with his scientific investigations. As a teenager she became interested in astronomy and won fame when she discovered a new comet in 1847. From 1849 she was employed as an astronomer by the US government. She was the first woman to be elected to the American Academy of Arts and Sciences, and was also president of the American Association for the Advancement of Women, and gave special help to other women scientists.

Elizabeth Cary Agassiz (1822–1907)

Born in Boston, Cary Agassiz married a Swiss naturalist, and worked with him studying marine biology. In 1865 she set out on a daring scientific expedition to Brazil via the dangerous waters off Cape Horn. She also took part in pioneer voyages to dredge up scientific samples from the sea bed.
In 1879 she became secretary of a group campaigning for a top-quality university for women. This was set up as Radcliffe College in 1893, and she became its first president.

Charlotte Cushman (1816–1876)

Theatre and dance were careers in which women often found fame and fortune. Cushman trained as an opera singer, then became an actor and theatre manager. She worked in the USA and in Europe. Famous for her moving, powerful performances, she played male as well as female roles, all with great success. Off-stage, she was a forceful personality, and used her wealth and fame to help younger women start their careers in music, art and the theatre.

Louie Fuller (1862–1928)

Louie Fuller (above) began her career in the circus and music hall, but became interested in 'artistic' dance. She created a style that used flowing silk cloth, and magical light effects produced by machines that she invented. Many of her dances were based on the natural world, with names like *Fire* and *Clouds*. Her performances inspired many artists, especially in Europe.

Margaret Fuller (1810–1850)

Fuller (below) was given a strict, academic education from her father. After he died in 1835, she became friends with many advanced thinkers, and arranged a famous series of discussion groups, where men and women met to debate important topics. In 1842 she became editor of a newspaper, *The Dial*, which supported equality for women and for slaves. She also wrote newspaper articles and a book on women's history. In 1847 she travelled to Italy, where she fell in love with an Italian nobleman and became active in Italian politics. In 1850 she decided to return to America with her husband and child, but their ship was wrecked in a storm, and she was drowned.

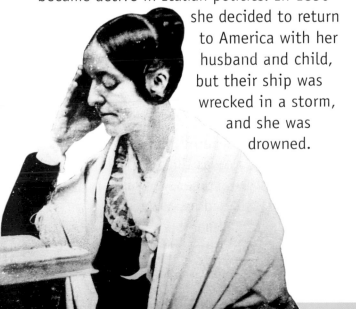

Louisa May Alcott (1832–1888)

Writer Louisa May Alcott (below) was the daughter of a philosopher. She was raised in poverty after her father's experimental vegetarian community failed. She helped make ends meet by sewing, teaching and working as a maid. From the age of 16, to earn money, she started writing stories and selling them to magazines. She worked as a nurse during the Civil War, then returned home to support her whole family by writing. In 1868 she wrote a children's book, *Little Women*, which became a best seller. She was active in the black civil rights and votes for women movements.

Mary Cassatt (1845–1926)

Cassatt was inspired to paint after a visit to Europe with her family, aged only six years. She studied art in America, but disliked the course and left to work in France. In 1877 the famous French artist Degas invited her to join a pioneer group of painters, known as the Impressionists. As the subjects of her pictures, Cassatt chose ordinary women and children, and household life – themes usually ignored by men painters. Between 1891 and 1892 she created a huge wall-painting for the Women's Building at the World Exposition (Exhibition) in Chicago. She continued to paint and draw until 1912, when she became almost blind.

Ernestine Rose (1810–1892)

Born in Poland, Ernestine Rose was the daughter of a rabbi. She arrived in the USA aged 26. She was strong minded and independent and soon became involved in many causes, including anti–slavery, socialism, and women's rights. She took legal action against her father, to try and win back money left to her by her mother, which her father had offered to another man if he married Ernestine. She was a forceful public speaker, and worked closely with Susan B Anthony, helping to organize meetings and petitions. She spent 12 years, between 1848 and 1860, campaigning for changes in the laws that governed married women's property rights and divorce.

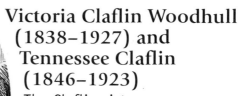

Victoria Claflin Woodhull (1838–1927) and Tennessee Claflin (1846–1923)

The Claflin sisters were campaigners for women's votes. Born into a poor family, they became successful businesswomen. They published a women's newspaper full of outrageous opinions. Most of all, they shocked the American public by openly discussing sex. At first women's rights leaders welcomed their help. But some women found that their behaviour was damaging the cause. When Victoria (above) declared that she would run for president in 1872, Susan B Anthony realized this would make the women's movement look ridiculous, and asked her to resign.

Mary Harris Jones (1830–1930)

'Mother' Jones was born in Ireland, but arrived in America aged five. She worked as a teacher and dressmaker, but then tragedy struck. Her husband and four children died in an epidemic, and she lost everything she owned in a fire that swept through Chicago in 1871. She returned to work, and became active in the trade union movement, organizing workers on railways and in mines. She also ran classes, to teach people about welfare and their rights. In 1900, aged 70, she organized marches for striking coalminers' wives in Virginia, and led a group of miners' children to the president's home. She was still attending union meetings at the age of 91.

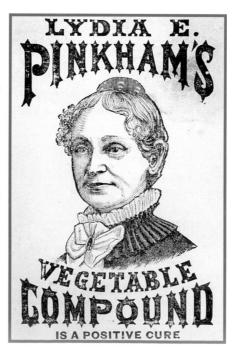

LYDIA E. PINKHAM'S VEGETABLE COMPOUND IS A POSITIVE CURE

Lydia E Pinkham (1819–1883)

Pinkham combined women's traditional healing remedies with new sales techniques. After her husband's business failed in 1873, she began to sell bottles of a mixture of herbs, roots and seeds, which she soaked and then brewed in her own kitchen. She said that women should drink three spoonfuls a day. Bottles of Pinkham's mixture carried her picture, and were printed with messages such as 'The Health of Women is the Hope of the Race'. Advertisements invited women to write to her for advice. By 1881 sales of Pinkham's mixture totalled almost $200 000 a year. Pinkham supported anti–slavery, temperance and women's rights.

Sarah Breedlove Walker (1867–1919)

Born in Louisiana, the daughter of black farmworkers, Sarah Breedlove Walker was orphaned aged six. She married at 14 and was widowed, with a child, by 20. She survived by working as a washerwoman, but also found time to study. She created a range of beauty products especially for black women, and became very rich. Madam Walker was a caring employer, setting up welfare schemes for her staff, and giving money to many charities. She also supported black people's rights.

'Calamity Jane' (1852–1903)

Calamity Jane was born as Martha Jane Cannary, daughter of frontier farmers. Dressed as a man, she worked skinning mules, then tried to join the US Army but was discovered to be a woman and sent home. She lived with outlaw Wild Bill Hickok, and had his child. After he was murdered, she gained a reputation for drunkenness and immorality. Although many people condemned her behaviour, she also won praise for nursing Sioux (Dakota) families through a smallpox outbreak – even though the Sioux were at war with US soldiers and settlers, and smallpox was a killer disease. From 1893 she supported herself by performing in Wild West shows.

Ida Lewis (born 1842)

Lewis (above) was a lighthouse-keeper's daughter. When she was 15 she took over running the lighthouse, after her father became ill. In 1859 (and again in 1869) she set out in icy, stormy seas to rescue boatmen in trouble. *Harper's* magazine, writing about the rescue, pointed out that: 'No man will be such a – let us say donkey – to insist that it was unfeminine in Ida Lewis to pull off in her boat to save men from drowning.' In 1879 she was awarded a Gold Medal for bravery, and allowed to become the official keeper of the lighthouse.

Antoinette Brown Blackwell (1825–1921)

Brown Blackwell was the first female minister of religion in the USA. She studied religion at Oberlin College, but at first no church would ordain her. Finally the Congregational Church agreed to let her serve as a minister from 1852 to 1854. Blackwell was active in anti-slavery and women's rights campaigns. She caused an outcry in 1853 when she protested against being banned from speaking – because she was a woman – to an international meeting of the worldwide temperance campaign.

Mary Baker Eddy (1821–1910)

Having being unwell for many years, Mary Baker Eddy found relief from constant pain after reading the Bible. She began to give lectures on healing, and published a book, *Science and Health*. In 1876 she set up the Christian Science Association, and in 1879 the First Church of Christ Scientist. This new religious movement grew rapidly, and spread to many countries beyond the USA.

GLOSSARY

abolition In 19th-century USA, abolition had the special meaning of ending slavery.

Amendment A change made to the US Constitution.

campaign An organized group of activities, such as speeches or marches, designed to change people's views or win new rights. (To campaign is to take part in a campaign.)

citizen A person who is a member of a community and has political rights within it.

civilize To make a person (or place) less wild and better behaved.

civil rights The rights that allow an ordinary person to play a full part in society, such as the right to vote, receive an education, have a job, marry and follow their own religious faith.

colony Land ruled by another, stronger country for its own benefit.

committee A group of people who meet to discuss important topics and make decisions.

conference A large meeting where people from many places meet to discuss topics of shared interest.

Congress The national law-making assembly of the USA. It is made up of two chambers, the **Senate** and the House of Representatives. Both have to agree on all new laws.

constitution A collection of laws that sets out the way a country is run.

corset A piece of clothing that made a woman's waist look slimmer by binding it tightly.

culture A society's customs, beliefs and artistic traditions.

debate A public discussion between people who hold opposing views.

declaration A public statement.

economy The financial affairs of a country.

election The process of voting for members of a government or other organization.

equality Having the same rights and opportunities, and being treated with respect.

family planning Limiting the number of children in a family.

feminist Someone who wants women to have equal rights and equal opportunities with men.

free speech Being able to express opinions without fear of being punished.

frontier In 19th-century USA, the boundary between settled land and wild countryside.

guardianship The legal right to look after a person.

idealist Someone who aims to improve the world.

immigrant Someone who leaves one country to make a new life in another.

immorality Behaviour that is not ruled by any kind of belief.

juror A member of the public who sits in a law court to decide whether someone is guilty of a crime.

law case A matter brought to court for discussion.

legal rights Rights that can be demanded by law.

lobby To present a group's views to a member of government.

missionary society An organization that collects money and sends religious teachers to work in different parts of society.

moral reform Improving people's behaviour towards one another.

oppression Unfair treatment by someone who has more power.

petition A document containing a list of demands. (To petition is to ask for changes to be made or needs to be met.)

piecework A system of producing goods where a worker is paid for each finished item.

pioneer Someone who explores or settles new land, or who develops new ideas or inventions.

prejudice Unfair or unbalanced opinions.

protest A demand for change. A protester is someone who demands change.

public office A job in national or local government.

Quaker A member of the religious movement called the Society of Friends. They have no priests and few organized services. Many Quaker women were leading social reformers.

rally An open-air march or meeting by a large number of people.

reforms Changes that bring improvements.

republic A country ruled by a government elected by the people.

Senate Part of the US government. Members of the senate (senators) discuss and vote on new laws.

socialist Someone who believes in a system of government in which ordinary people have a say in how their country is run.

state funds Money from the government.

suffrage The right to vote in political elections. A suffragist is someone who believes in extending suffrage to more people.

sweatshop A crowded, unhealthy workroom.

temperance Not drinking alchohol.

trade union A group of workers who have joined together to demand better pay and working conditions.

wagon trail Trackways used by covered wagons making the journey to the far west of the USA.

welfare scheme An organized plan to improve people's living conditions, providing better health care and everyday support.

women's rights The rights of women to be equal with men in society.

FURTHER READING

The Macmillan Dictionary of Women's Biography (Macmillan, 2nd edition, 1989)
The Young Oxford History of Women in the United States (OUP, 11 volumes, by order only)

INDEX